The *Inspirational* Story of

JELLY POE

The *Inspirational* Story of

JELLY POE

With insight from Jelly Poe's Dad, Moh L. Poe

Dr. Kevin LaChapelle

iUniverse

THE INSPIRATIONAL STORY OF JELLY POE
WITH INSIGHT FROM JELLY POE'S DAD, MOH L. POE

iUniverse books may be ordered through booksellers or by contacting:

iUniverse
1663 Liberty Drive
Bloomington, IN 47403
www.iuniverse.com
1-800-Authors (1-800-288-4677)

Because of the dynamic nature of the Internet, any web addresses or links contained in this book may have changed since publication and may no longer be valid. The views expressed in this work are solely those of the author and do not necessarily reflect the views of the publisher, and the publisher hereby disclaims any responsibility for them.

Any people depicted in stock imagery provided by Getty Images are models, and such images are being used for illustrative purposes only.
Certain stock imagery © Getty Images.

ISBN: 978-1-5320-4667-4 (sc)
ISBN: 978-1-5320-4669-8 (hc)
ISBN: 978-1-5320-4668-1 (e)

New American Standard Bible (NASB) Copyright © 1960, 1962, 1963, 1968, 1971, 1972, 1973, 1975, 1977, 1995 by The Lockman Foundation

Print information available on the last page.

iUniverse rev. date: 06/23/2018

Contents

Chapter One

The Karen People

Jelly Poe was the epitome of his Karen community and his strong Karen values. As the Karen are known for their kind hearts and gentle nature, Jelly exuded these values and then some. His influence was unfathomable. If you ask anyone who knew Jelly, even for a short time, they will likely tell you how he impacted them and changed their life!

When I first met Jelly through Facebook in late 2016

to early 2017, I was immediately struck by the polite and authentic tone in his messages to me. Jelly was very proud of the outreach projects that we were doing in Karen State. He would tell me, "Sir, I am very proud of you and your team!" By following our posts, he was aware of many details of the work we were doing with his people.

You might be wondering, who are the Karen people, and what is their story? According to historians, the Karen people once lived in the heart of civilization near the Tigris and Euphrates Rivers. When the Syrians took control of the Babylonian empire, the Karen first moved toward central Asia, then to Mongolia, then down south through the Gobi Desert, an area they described as a very green country from generation to generation. They remained there in the western part of China for some time before continuing south to the Yunnan province of China.

In about 1300 BC, the combination of drought and ethnic pressure drove the Karen into Thailand and Burma along the three great rivers, the Mekong, the Salween, and the Irrawaddy.

Then they settled in the Irrawaddy delta region

and are believed to have been the first ethnic group to populate Myanmar, the country formerly known as Burma. About three hundred years after the Karen settled in Burma, the people now described as the Burmese emigrated west from India and settled in. The Burmese began to oppress and fight the Karen, burning down their villages, killing family members, and torturing them, The Karen had to flee for their lives into the mountains and into the thick jungles.

So, for centuries, the Karen people have been fighting desperately for their land and their culture, even when control of the area changed from one nation to another. They suffered oppression under the Burmese kings with some being executed just because they were literate.

Their situation improved somewhat under British rule because all ethnic groups were supposed to be treated fairly. But during World War II, when the Japanese controlled Burma, the brutality against the Karen people was in full force. Women were raped, and villages were destroyed by Burmese because the Karen people remained loyal to the British with hopes of gaining their own state. After World War II, the British made Burma independent, but the Karen continued to suffer under Burmese leadership.

The Karen had been betrayed by Britain, and now would face the brutality of the Burmese leaders. The Karen are very trusting, and take people for their word, because that is how the Karen people are. Unfortunately, Burma over and over takes advantage and exploits the Karen for their trust they place in others.

In early February 1947, the Karen National Union (KNU) was formed at a Karen Congress. Seven hundred delegates from the Karen National Associations, both Christian, Animist, and Buddhist attended the meeting. The KNU's mission is to lead the fight for the freedom and human rights of not only the Karen people, but all the ethnic groups in Burma, and to achieve harmony, peace, stability, and prosperity for all.

However, in 1949, violence against the Karen people escalated and continues in what is said to be the longest-running internal war in history. Many have fled the country to escape being killed, tortured, raped, and/or or enslaved by the brutal and corrupt Burmese military regime. Some refugees live in camps along the Thai border; many have resettled in the United States.

So how did I become aware of the Karen and Jelly Poe?

In 2011, I had the good fortune of meeting some of the most amazing people in San Diego, California, I had ever encountered. These were no ordinary people. A community group reached out to me sharing that a group of refugees from Karen State were targeted by local street gangs on their way home from school. These high school students barely spoke English and were small in stature. Many feared the young Karen people might succumb to the pressure to join the gangs as a means of protecting themselves.

I was sent a YouTube video, which had gone viral, of the Karen defending themselves from the gang members who attacked them on their way home from school one day, but the street hoodlums were in for a rude awakening. The Karen had experienced a tough life, and their fascination with martial arts did not bode well for the gang members who only knew how to street-fight. The Karen defended themselves with roundhouse kicks, and after a short time, the gang members began to realize that these "small" guys were very strong and determined not to allow the abuse to continue. Then instead of attacking the Karen teenagers, they tried to recruit them. The street hoodlums figured the Karen fighting skills could help them defend their turf. I knew all too well the psychology of gangs as that was my expertise when I was a police officer. I knew I had to provide intervention strategies quickly to prevent this from happening.

I began to research the Karen State to learn of the history. I wanted to know what these young people experienced so I would have insight on how best to impact them. The more I learned about the history of the Karen people, the more I became frustrated and saddened by what the Karen had endured for decades. They had experienced such violence that most were not willing to share because it was so painful.

Many groups have advocated for the Karen people; one such group is the Free Burma Rangers led by David Eubank. David and his team have done incredible work to not only reduce suffering but empower the Karen people to become trained medics. Not only would they be able to help their own people, they would be trained to help their newfound friends to be resilient in their fight for freedom. For example, when David was called to action in Syria, he brought with him Karen people David has mentored and trained over the years as field medics. Though other groups have also worked for many years standing alongside the Karen people, the Karen seemed most proud of the Free Burma Rangers because of David and his family being so loyal to their calling. David, his wife, and their kids were no stranger to danger. They were on the front lines. I can remember when I asked Jelly Poe if he had seen the video I posted on Facebook that captured David Eubank running directly in the line of fire to save a little girl in Syria. Jelly had seen it, and we talked about David and his family's incredible faith and how David and his family have impacted thousands and thousands of lives.

The Karen people had come to America seeking refuge, and they were once again the target of violence perpetrated against them by no fault of their own, from the local street gangs. I knew all too well the callousness of the gangs and how their potential to destroy Karen families by capturing the hearts of their young.

So, I moved quickly and formed a Karen Leadership Academy through a nonprofit I founded in 1999, PowerMentor. The first Karen I encountered were Chit

Tway, Eh De Gray, El Dale, Shmoh Lah (now known as Samuel Thaw), Thaw So, and Ler Doh. As we began to talk, they shared their history and what their people had endured and continue to endure at the hands of the Burmese army. I was so moved by the intelligence of these young people, their courage, and the fact that they were very articulate. I remember asking them what their life's purpose was. They told me from day one that the believed God called them to return to their country and help their Karen people. I was astonished to hear such an articulate and thoughtful response. I was so moved to stand with them.

I took them to National University where I taught, so they could share their story with my graduate students. My students were completely stunned by the Karen team I brought to class, and absolutely speechless when they heard about the brutal attacks the Karen people endured from the Burmese army for decades.

Many people around them mocked the idea that these young Karen wanted to return to their land to help their people, telling them they could never do that. I could see that many treated them as victims, while we saw them as victors. I told them I was committed to helping the Karen people and would stand with them and go with them back to their country.

The more I learned about the Karen people, the more awed and inspired I became. They were very kind, considerate, well mannered, and forgiving, especially considering what they had endured all their lives.

I also noted that anyone who encountered Karen people was very impacted by their influence. From schoolteachers, to community members, the Karen would quickly earn a reputation of being the most kindhearted people ever! The Karen culture was so strong. They loved God, their families, and their community. And perhaps the tassels on their clothing played a role in their extraordinary kindness.

Traditional Karen shirts and skirts often feature tassels. It is said that they are never to be removed because of a reference in the Bible: "Make for themselves tassels on the corners of their garments

9

throughout their generations, and that they shall put on the tassel of each corner a cord of blue. It shall be a tassel for you to look at and remember all the commandments of the LORD, so as to do them and not follow after your own heart and your own eyes, after which you played the harlot, so that you may remember to do all My commandments and be holy to your God. I am the LORD your God who brought you out from the land of Egypt to be your God; I am the LORD your God" (Numbers 15:38–41 NASB)

Jelly Poe took that kindness to the next level! He would later share with me how important he thought it was for Karen young people to go back to their country to help their people. He felt it was kind and the right thing to do. He shared with me his wish to go with us one day.

Fast forward to 2014, and I would lead the first trip back to Karen State to assess the situation, the vulnerabilities, and the opportunities for future trips with our team. But the Karen members of our team were not yet able to go as they were awaiting their U.S. citizenship documents.

During our first trip, I assembled a group that would

could help us set the foundation for future annual trips to Karen State. I was joined by Andrew Trueblood, a former master's student of mine who had previous experience in the U.S. Marine Corps and a master's in Asian Pacific studies. Andrew was incredibly knowledgeable of the political history of the region and possessed a high level of situational awareness that I knew I would need for us to be effective in our objectives. He was also a very hard worker and very operationally solid. He was the guy you knew you could count on. Next was Darin Berlin. Also, one of my former graduate students, Darin brought with him incredible relationship skills. Darin was able to immerse himself into a culture, building high trust relationships, and was no stranger to world travel. Darin loved traveling the world even solo at times. He brought amazing skills to the team. Next was Tom Pham whom I had met at Sharp HealthCare where he worked in the lab. Tom was an incredible asset as he was very strong and also picked up language and cultural norms very quickly, adapting himself to the environment in a unique way. He brings the best out in others, is humble and a reliable team member. Next was Anthony Corona, known for his dutifulness and hard work. Anthony had accompanied me on many other trips over the years such as El Salvador, Mexico, and others. He was motivated by duty rather than desire. He was a tough nut to crack, yet, if he was tempered he would be a hard worker.

Jelly was very worried about his Karen people knowing that tough times lie ahead for the Karen who lived in their Karen State, and in the camps that were bursting at the seams with restricted resources from international aid agencies. Jelly and his family knew all too well the challenges experienced by the Karen in the refugee camps.

His family knew what life was like in the refugee camps and were one of the lucky families who were able to immigrate to the United States. But they had no idea what life in the States would also bring heartbreak— their firstborn son would be with them for a short time.

Chapter Two

Life in Mae La Refugee Camp

Moh L. Poe, Jelly's dad, was born in a village called Lere Ger Day. Around 1990, Moh was forced out of his village and sought refuge at Mae La refugee camp in Thailand. His mom, My Thaw Say, who was born in Htee Ko refugee camp. She also relocated to Mae La. While living at Mae La, Moh L. Poe and My Thaw

Say married and began their family with the birth of their firstborn son, Jelly. In 2002, their daughter, Hen Nay Thaw and their second son, Lah Bywe Htoo, and finally their fourth and last child, Johnantha, who was born in the USA, Smyrna, Tennessee.

Mae La refugee camp in Thailand was established in 1984 in Tha Song Yang District, Tak Province in the Dawna Range area. Currently, it is home to more than 60,000 refugees and is the largest camp. The first refugees arrive in 1984, mostly of the Karen or Karenni ethnicities, fleeing armed conflict and ethnic persecution by the Burmese government.

The Burmese army burned to the ground thousands of villages, especially in the Karen and Karenni States—houses, churches, schools, belongings, and sometimes even domestic animals. The army directly attacked the Karen people, placing them into forced labor or enslaving them, destroying not only their homes but also their crops.

Since Mae La is considered an educational center for refugees, the current population includes several thousand students who come to study in the camp (some from other camps but mostly from Burma).

However, the schools hold no formal accreditation. After graduating, students are often left with credentials that are not recognized by the Thai or Burmese governments, leaving them feeling duped.

Periodically during 2004 and 2005, Thai authorities allowed Burmese refugees to register with the United Nations High Commissioner for Refugees (UNHCR. And since 2005, all registered refugees have been eligible for resettlement to third countries. Nearly 80 percent of the refugees were Karen, 10 percent were Karenni; all were originally from eastern Burma. In June 2014, 96,206 had been resettled; 75 percent of them headed to the United States, followed by Australia, Canada, Finland, and Norway. Resettlement numbers declined each year since 2008 since most of the registered refugees had already left. The group settlement program to the United States closed in 2014, with those refugees in the pipeline departing in 2015.

According to Bio-Med Central International Health and Human Rights organization, around 400,000 Karen people are without housing, and 128,000 are living in camps on the Thailand-Burma border. Most refugees remain within the confines of the camps; they risk being arrested by the Thai police if they leave. So, employment for the Karen refugees is scarce and risky. Former refugee Hla Wah said, "There were no jobs, so if the adults wanted to work, they had to leave quietly without getting caught by Thai police." Wah lived in a camp called Nu Poe where she went to school and helped her parents care for the five brothers and four sisters. Though her parents worked sporadically out, they earned so little money, it wasn't worth the risk. Hla suffered from malnutrition because her parents did not have money to buy food for the family.

Jelly Poe remembered what it was like living in Mae La from his birth to about 2010. He was very intelligent and could see the challenges facing Karen State and his Karen people more so than most, especially for his age. During one of our many conversations, I shared with him a phenomenon that I saw in Karen State during a visit, particularly in the refugee camps. Young people in the refugee camps, because of their situation, see very little hope for their future because of the uncertainty of their lives. Many of them were born in the refugee camps and some have been there for twenty plus years. If we use the analogy of fleas inside a jar. You can place the lid on the jar and the fleas are going to fly around, and they're going to stay within that jar and become acclimated to this jar. The jar symbolizes the refugee camp.

And so even if you remove the lid, the fleas won't even attempt to fly out because they have been acclimated to the lid as a ceiling, and will not even attempt to fly out, and they will stay within the confines of that jar. And should you dump the fleas out of the jar, the fleas will still fly in formation as if they are still enclosed in the jar, taking the exact shape of the jar. They become acclimated to that shape, and it will take quite a bit of time for the fleas to begin to realize that they're actually no longer confined.

Here's the point I made to Jelly: When you are in the refugee camps, it's critical for you to train your mind to begin seeing yourself as a leader in the future and the things that you can do to help people and develop yourself. You cannot see yourself stuck in the refugee camp. For the moment, when you are in the camp, your life may be in a holding pattern, so you can develop yourself as best as you possibly can. So, when doors open in the future, even if you don't know which doors may open, but trust me, there are doors that will open, you'll be able to step through them and be fully prepared. This really resonated with Jelly.

We also talked about how many times people trap themselves and are not able to grow because they will not let go. Since Jelly loved listening to stories, I shared with him a story about the methods used to trap monkeys in some countries. One method is to fasten a hollow container such a vase with a small opening, and put some nuts, berries, or fruit in the hole as bait.

And what happens is this: The monkey comes along and smells the bait. The monkey says, "Wow. This is great. I found some food." So, it scopes things out, makes its hand as narrow as possible to make it fit through that narrow passageway. The monkey grabs the nuts, berries, or fruit. And now, it makes a fist to hold on to the nuts and berries in its hand. And now the monkey can't get its hand out. It's trapped!

What's interesting is: All the monkey has to do is simply let go, and it would be free. Instead, it will not let go. It hangs on to the nuts, berries, fruit, but they are nothing in comparison to its life. Yet, the monkey hangs on to it and basically forfeit its life.

This story made Jelly think. How many times in life do we hang on to certain things? We hang on for dear life, and that's the one thing that's either holding us back, or the one thing that's trapping us. And this could come in the form of our friends that maybe we shouldn't be around, a significant other, maybe a job that's holding us back, maybe the place that we are at in life.

Jelly, of course, quickly understood the analogy and principle involved. We agreed it is best to just let go, and let God, and watch the amazing things that can happen in our life.

In December 2017, when PowerMentor went to Mae La Camp, it had an entirely new meaning for our team. We dedicated Project Kawthoolei 2017–2018 to Jelly Poe, and when I entered the camp, it was different than past years. This time, I tried to look through the lens of Jelly Poe. When I was drawn to the stories of the young people who felt despair, I shared with them about a special person who was my hero, and his name was Jelly Poe.

A Call to Action

Jelly would later call me to action to stand for his

Karen people. He was very insightful and was very concerned how the world seemed to overlook the continual human rights violations against the Karen and other ethnic nationalities in the region. Jelly would wonder how other governments would send money to Burma, when they were just using the money to go after the ethnic groups. In fact, he was incensed that the overt statement of the Burma Army was to remove all remnants of the ethnic groups, all language, culture, and religion. In fact, one general made a public state that in 20-years the Karen would only be found in museums. We would talk about the desire of the Burma Army to Burmanize the entire region, and they would not stop. They hated Christians, which was the largest religions group of the Karen, and the violations continue even to today.

I would later be taught by Jelly very specific details that would compel me to do more and more for his Karen people, the injustice has been horrible.

Chapter Three

Coming to America

Jelly's family was fortunate to be accepted to the resettlement program, allowing them to move to the United States in December 2010. Kaw Khu remembers all too well when Jelly's family arrived in America because he served as their translator and to help them navigate their new life in a new country.

Coming to the States posed a challenge in and of itself. The Poe family had never seen modern conveniences such as a sink with running water, a bathroom with a toilet and shower, appliances like a stove, refrigerator, or microwave oven, navigated through traffic in a city, in addition to getting acclimated to their new life. They arrived by plane in Nashville, and then journeyed by car to Smyrna, Tennessee, where they made a two-bedroom apartment their home. They had to learn how to use all of the modern devices to cook and clean. Life in Tennessee was so different than life in the camp!

Many Karen laughed when they saw the modern amenities. They were surprised that people did not just go the creek to get water and hunt to find food. But the Karen people faced other challenges after seeking refuge in the United States. While some Americans were drawn to the amazing Karen culture, others would see the young Karen students and make fun of them for not speaking English or their small stature.

This was heartbreaking for many who fell in love with the Karen. They found it hard to believe or accept that gangsters picked on the amazing Karen. But Jelly seemed to escape these issues. He knew others who were enduring prejudice and non-acceptance, but he found the community of Smyrna, Tennessee, to be very supportive and welcoming. From the onset, he earned the support of his fellow Karen families, his schoolteachers, and his soccer colleagues.

Jelly was bothered by the incident that drew me to the Karen. He was very troubled that young Karen in San Diego had to endure those hardships. He told me,

"That was not kind of them to do that." Jelly had his simple approach and response to things he viewed as not right.

From early on in his life, Jelly embraced the positive in everything. He often shared with me that leading a simple life and being kind to everyone was the only way to live. He figured everyone should know that. When I told Jelly that he was very unique, "He would say, no, sir, I just try to be kind to others and I am thankful to Jesus for everything."

I often discussed with Jelly the concerns I had that some young Karen would use alcohol to escape their hurts in life. I asked him what he thought when he witnessed some of his teenage friends hanging out and drinking. But he responded with, "It is hard to see that, sir. But one day, they will see it is not the way to be." I noted that he never talked down or negatively about those who chose to engage in that behavior. He was mature beyond his years.

He would share with me how he got along with everyone and he felt that was because he was kind to everyone, never talked bad about people, and always wore a smile. That seemed to be his simple mantra in his life.

Jelly was concerned with what he perceived as an increase in divorce or separation among the Karen people. We talked about how this was never an issue back home. But for some reason, he began to hear about these family breakups, it really bothered him, especially Sar's.

Twenty-three-year-old Sar was also a refugee from Karen State. He was now living in Fort Wayne, Indiana. He posted his life's motto on his Facebook page: "To become a good man, what do you have to do? Believe God, worship God, follow God, help others in need, stay out the trouble, follow the law, and be a helper in your community." To me, Sar seemed like a modern-day version of the Joseph in Genesis 37–39. Sar's story and Joseph's story were eerily similar. And I shared my reflections and the parallels with Jelly, who loved to listen to Bible stories.

In the Bible, God favored Joseph. His brothers were jealous of his success and had left him to die in a pit. Some Ishmaelites found Joseph and sold him to an Egyptian named Potiphar, who was the captain of the pharoah's bodyguard. Potiphar made Joseph his household slave. Potiphar saw that "the LORD was with him and *how* the LORD caused all that he did to prosper in his hand. So Joseph found favor in his sight and became his personal servant; and he made him overseer over his house, and all that he owned he put in his charge. It came about that from the time he made him overseer in his house and over all that he owned, the LORD blessed the Egyptian's house on account of Joseph; thus the LORD's blessing was upon all that he owned, in the house and in the field. So, he left everything he owned in Joseph's charge; and with him *there* he did not concern himself with anything except the food which he ate" (Genesis 39, NASB).

After some time, Potiphar's wife began to desire Joseph, because he was well built and handsome. One day, she asked him to sleep with her. He refused, saying, "my master does not concern himself with anything in the house, and he has put all that he owns in my charge. There is no one greater in this house than I, and he has withheld nothing from me except you because you are his wife. How then could I do this great evil and sin against God?" (Genesis 39, NASB).

Notwithstanding, Potipher's wife talked to Joseph every day, trying to seduce him, but he refused to have sexual relations with her or even spend time with her. Joseph had the wisdom to know that she was not a good thing, and definitely not from the Lord.

One day, Joseph went into the house to do his work as usual and was the only man in the house at that time. Potipher's wife grabbed his coat and said to him, "Lie with me." But Joseph ran out of the house, leaving his coat in her hand. "When she saw that he had left his garment in her hand and had fled outside, she called to the men of her household and said to them, 'See, he has brought in a Hebrew to us to make sport of us; he came in to me to lie with me, and I screamed. When he heard that I raised my voice and screamed, he left his garment beside me and fled and went outside.' So, she left his garment beside her until his master came home. Then she spoke to him with these words, 'The Hebrew slave, whom you brought to us, came in to me to make sport of me; and as I raised my voice and screamed, he left his garment beside me and fled outside'" (Genesis 39, NASB).

When Potiphar heard what his wife said Joseph had

done, he became very angry. Potiphar arrested Joseph and put him into prison with the other prisoners of the king. But the Lord was with Joseph and showed him kindness and caused the prison warden to like Joseph. The prison warden chose Joseph to take care of all the prisoners, and he was responsible for whatever was done in the prison. "The chief jailer did not supervise anything under Joseph's charge because the LORD was with him; and whatever he did, the LORD made to prosper" (Genesis 39, NASB).

Like Joseph, God also favored Sar. He was successful, a hard worker, owned a home, was married, had one little boy, and served as the stepdad for his wife's son from her first marriage. Many said of Sar, "Wow, everything he puts his hands on is successful."

Many religious leaders also thought highly of Sar, and they warned him about his intended wife. Her reputation was not good, and there were stories circulating about her conduct during her first marriage. But Sar was the type of person who always gave others the benefit of the doubt, and he saw the best in them as well, so he did not take into account their warnings about the woman he wanted to marry.

Some I have talked to felt that like Joseph, Sar was seduced by his wife; she knew that he was a hard worker and naive according to many who had known him for a long time. Sadly, Sar would later reflect that he should have known better. Intellectually he realized that his wife was not the person for him, but emotionally he gave in. His decision would change his life forever in the worst way.

Sar and his wife had a son together. Sar treated both boys equally, as if his stepson was his very own. Soon he began to see things changing. At first, his wife seemed interested in helping their church and their community. But little by little, Sar would begin to see his wife's selfishness and her desire for more possessions. She became frustrated that Sar chose to help others with his hard-earned money. As time went on, Sar's wife wanted to work, so she could have even more things. Sar hoped that she would stay home with the boys, but she was persistent.

When Sar's wife got a job, things began to change at a more rapid pace. Sar would later learn that his wife was drawn into a sexual relationship with a woman she had met at work. This woman was into very bad things;

she had been arrested for selling drugs. Sar's family was being torn apart, and he felt helpless. At one point, his wife became violent and tried to stab him. But when the police came, he did not want to prosecute, hoping to rebuild their relationship. Sar sought help from their family pastor as well.

Like Potiphar's wife's deceptive and callous behavior, Sar's wife would allege that Sar forced her to go to their pastor, and she and her girlfriend concocted a story that Sar kidnapped her. They devised a plan to remove him from the picture: get him arrested for kidnapping, obtain a restraining order, and then take all of his assets—home, cars, savings accounts, etc.—while he sat in jail. Then Sar's wife and her new girlfriend could live happily ever after with the two boys, while Sar was awaiting trial for kidnapping, which could potentially carry a ten-year prison sentence.

Sar was devastated. How could the Lord allow this to happen to him? His wife's parents would mock him. They could boast in the community and especially to Sar's parents and relatives how their daughter got Sar arrested and how he would lose everything.

While Sar was in jail, God had His hand on Sar,

giving him favor with all of the other prisoners and guards, just like Joseph in the Bible. Many times, when I was on the phone with Sar, he was singing with joy in his heart, and I could hear him encouraging other prisoners. Sar even was able to encourage all of the inmates in his cell block to attend church on Sunday. The guards took special note of this. The guards could see something was very different about Sar: The prisoners acted differently when Sar was present. Sar was not a normal prisoner: he was nothing like the ones they were accustomed to seeing in jail. Of course, Sar had his moments of struggles and doubt. He and I spent many calls praying together and crying together asking God for strength. The bottom line, instead of his ex-wife harming him, God used that situation to build Sar into a stronger person and gave him the opportunity to encourage people at the most vulnerable time in their lives. Sar would now reflect on life, and the lessons he has learned. Eventually, Sar was released from jail and placed on probation as he could not afford to fight the bogus charges. They divorced, after Sar was released from jail. Now, Sar knows that his focus is to care for his sons and serve his Karen people.

I count it a privilege to have walked alongside of Sar with his Pastor Jo who never stopped believing in him. The lesson for families is to never take things for granted, and you had better make sure you know what you are doing when you enter into marriage. Ladies, make sure it is the right guy for you, and guys, make sure she is the right one for you.

Jelly felt very bad for Sar; he felt in his heart that Sar was wronged, and he wondered what would ever come of Sar. Jelly would encourage me to stand with Sar because as Jelly said, "It would be the kind thing to do."

Chapter Four

The Best Son and Brother

Jelly's mom knew her son was special, unlike most children. She noted how her firstborn was so different from most kids. When she told Jelly that he could not do something, such as go out with his friends, he never argued, and always accepted the direction he was given by his parents. Kaw Khu, the translator assigned to the Poe family, always noticed how well-behaved Jelly was and how much he respected others. Kaw said it was so different from most other kids. Hee enjoyed so much helping Jelly's family, whether it meant writing a check to pay rent, or translating English documents for them. It was always a joy to be around Jelly.

Jelly's siblings looked up to him, and they knew there was something very special about their big brother. He was their protector, their nurturer, and he led them by example. His mom and dad recognized from the onset, that Jelly was no ordinary son. He was unique, of course, and as their firstborn, he had an even more special bond with them.

Jelly loved his parents so much. He often told me how he had the best parents in the world. He knew that they loved him and his siblings, and he deeply appreciated all the sacrifices they had made for all of them. He was keenly aware of what they suffered back in their country, and he knew there were many things they did not share with him that scarred their hearts. Jelly would reflect many times as to what his parents had to endure, and he really worried about his Karen people.

Jelly knew that his parents were very proud of him and that intrinsically motivated him deep inside. He knew that they could sense how special Jelly was. Jelly had such strong faith in the Lord knowing that his parents were preselected to provide guidance, nurture, and discipline for him as he was brought into this world, and through all of the tough and amazing times they shared. He had remarkable faith and trust in God and in God's will for his life.

Jelly was known to never question his parents, when they gave him instruction, he listened and was very obedient. He was the same with his Lord. I would share his story in many Karen communities, sharing how he trusted his parents completely, and knew they had his interest at heart always. Jelly knowing that the Lord had ordained his parents and appointed them to lead him through his life. He was grateful, and I do not think I have ever seen such a young person so confident in this premise.

Jelly had tremendous empathy for young people who were getting into trouble. He seemed to sense that they did not have the perspective that he did in obeying his parents and the Lord. Jelly knew many young Karen young people in his own community were wandering into behavior that he knew was not good. I would ask him what he thought about young people getting into alcohol and drugs. He would say, "It is very sad, sir, they are going to get themselves in a lot of trouble." He would ask me how I would reach them if I could, and I would share with him different strategies, including the model, connect, and involve approach. Jelly was fascinated and wanted to learn more.

I explained that to be an effective leader, first, we must model positive behavior, and then we must connect with people in a very special way, and lastly, involve them in projects that show them a purpose and reveal their talent. I would share that this was the premise for our trips abroad to Kawthoolei. He was intrigued.

I also told Jelly that he had exceptional influence and that this was an amazing leadership characteristic for someone to possess at his young age. He would say, "You really think I have influence, sir?" I would share with him many times how much impact he was having on his community, family, and friends. I would also share the impact he had on my life. He would say, "That is very kind, sir."

Somehow Jelly knew he was not going to be on this earth for long. I could sense this whenever he talked to me. Many times Jelly would ask me over and over, "Sir, please never give up on our Karen people!" I would tell him, "Jelly, I promise you, I will never give up as long as I live." He would then tell me that he believed I was telling him the truth, and he believed that God sent me to the Karen people to stand with them.

Jelly and I would often talk about the legend of the lost books. Back in the early 1800s, missionaries traveled to Burma to convert the Karen people to Christianity. As they began teaching from the Bible, they were surprised to know that the Karen people already worshipped a god they called "Y'wa" and were familiar with the story of Creation and many other parts of the Old Testament. According to the legend, Y'wa gave the Karen people a golden book that represented the Bible and a silver book that represented education. The Buddhist, Christian and the Animists held slightly different variations of this legend. The silver book represented a white brother who would bring education to help free the Karen people, and many older Karen people believed that I was that white brother. The legend is said to be actual historical events, and many of the older Karen were very adamant about this.

Florence Poba-Prieto, a trusted Karen elder, and one of my close advisors, told me, "I think you, Kevin LaChapelle, are the Silver Book and the Karen will be the forefront for the rest of the ethnics. I have alerted

Burma and Thailand prayer groups to pray. Kevin, be courageous and know the good Lord is with you," she would tell me.

Eh Gay would share with many that he too believed that I was rising to teach and develop Karen leaders, and he felt this looked like the legend in their history. He shared that the Karen brother (Pu Day Wah or White Brother) who is said to bring back freedom for the Karen, restore their language and country Kawthoolei. Because our little brother Pu Day Wah who stole everything from the older brother (Karen). He has to payback. He then explained. Kevin LaChapelle we believe you are that one.

Many believed that I was fulfilling the white brother who would bring education or knowledge to the Karen. Perhaps I was well received by the Karen because I had a doctorate in education and was a professor teaching them leadership skills. The Karen tell me they have patiently waited for the gift of education to return to them, and they believe this person will raise up the young Karen to be leaders, and they believe I am fulfilling this legend, especially with my stated purpose of developing Karen leaders. At times, when Karen share this story with me, this is very emotional for me, sharing that they believe I can bring education needed by the Karen to rise up and free themselves from the bondage of the Burmese Army.

Jelly was intrigued by this, and would ask me, "Sir, maybe they are right, and you are called to the Karen people by God to help educate us and teach our young people to be leaders." I would have tears in my eyes as we would discuss this. I was humbled by this, and remained quiet, not knowing what to say. Yet, I felt this compelling desire to stand with the Karen at all cost, no matter what might be required of me.

Chapter Five

Jelly, the Student

Jenna Delaney Gibbons reflected that she was lucky enough to be Jelly's ESL (English as a Second Language) teacher at Smyrna Elementary when he arrived in Smyrna, at just eight-years-old. Jelly walked into her ESL classroom when he was in second grade. Little did she know that this boy would change her life forever. He had no clue what she was saying to him, but he came each and every day with his big, sweet smile. They sang songs, worked on vocabulary, learned letters/sounds, cooked recipes, did experiments, and had tons of fun. She had a very special connection with Jelly, and Jenna truly wanted the best for him! He learned quickly and was eager to learn as much as he could with the help of his friend, Moe Loe. Jenna knew then that this little boy was very special and extremely smart. He grew up and learned so much at school and always stopped to say hi to her when she saw him in the hallway.

Jelly impacted the lives of so many at his church. Felicia Smith Anderson shared that from the first time he walked through the church doors at Mission, he brought joy to everyone. One of Jelly's famous sayings was, "Hello, my brother from another mother, how are you?" Or, "Hello, my sister from another mother, how are you?" She reflected that she still can hear him saying it right now.

Kaw Khu recalls the times he would help out with Jelly as he was getting ready to school. He remembers the challenges Jelly family faced in getting food and finding work. Kaw was right there, and he loved Jelly and his family. Even today, Kaw stays very close to Jelly's family. Kaw knew all too well the challenges refugees would face in school, from bullying, to challenges in their studies.

Jelly was different. He escaped being bullied, I would say primarily because of his high likability. Everyone loved Jelly. It was extraordinary. Teachers and students alike would share with me how much Jelly impacted them through his example, and his ever so tender way about him. Jelly had a strong sense of humor, too. He would make people laugh and always wore his famous smile. He was described as such a gentleman, and I can only imagine, because he was so well spoken, always choosing his words carefully. He would always say "sir" and "ma'am," and he always spoke positive words, never cursed, never talked bad about others, and again, he was very compliant in class. Always following the instructions of his teachers. He knew very well they, too, had his interest at heart. He knew they were there to help him.

In and out of school, Jelly carried himself gently, yet confidently. He was very competitive, yet, possessed such amazing sportsmanship and character. Jelly was said to be well beyond his years. He was so mature, yet, his playfulness always impacted those he encountered. Everyone had a deep respect for him and a reverence, knowing that he was a "good kid" and that he was always trying to do the right thing.

Jelly could see the challenges his peers would face in life. He would tell me that God gave me favor with the young Karen and that I should travel to Karen communities across the United States to encourage them to fulfil their God-given purpose. He would ask me to commit to him that I would be faithful to do this. I would commit to him that yes, I would do this!

Chapter Six

Jelly, the Soccer Player

It did not take long for Jelly to make a name for himself on the soccer field. Jelly had such a gentle manner about him, but all that changed on the soccer field when he. His passion and energy would come alive. However, all those he played with noted that Jelly was different than the other soccer players. Competition on the field often turns to conflict and disregard for the other team's players. Not so with Jelly Poe. Jelly was an exceptional soccer player and athlete, pushing his limits, yet, his gentle words surfaced during games with his teammates and players from the opposing team. Who was this Jelly Poe and why was he so different?

Kaw Khu recanted how Jelly was so funny and one time he forgot his shoes for soccer and he called his mom to ask for the shoes, but his mom could not drive, so Kaw went to retrieve his shoes for him, and this happened several times, Jelly was all smiles, thought it was the funniest thing.

Jelly was so passionate about soccer. He was so anchored and never drifted from what he felt was his calling, to play soccer to the best of his ability. I remember sharing a story with him about when people drift in life and how important it is to be anchored to something important.

I began to share with Jelly a true story about sometimes how we drift, and we forget our anchor, our character, or what our purpose in life is. I recalled one time when I first moved from Colorado to San Diego. I was down at the ocean with my cousin, who was a surfer. I wanted to learn to surf but couldn't quite stand up on the board, so I used a boogie board instead. I was out floating around and pretty soon I heard a lifeguard yelling in his bullhorn out to the water, but I could not understand what he was saying. I thought, *what is this guy yelling?*

I just continued doing what I was doing, kind of swimming around there on the boogie board waiting for a wave, and the lifeguard did it again and again, a few more times, yelling through his bullhorn. Pretty soon, he just ran down to the water, put on his fins, and dove in. And I saw him swimming, dragging his red buoy, and swimming in my direction. I thought, *oh my God, someone's drowning right near me.* I started looking around, trying to find who might be in trouble so I could help that person if he or she was drowning. And I realized that the farther the lifeguard swam, the closer he was coming to me! Pretty soon, he looped around me and told me, "Grab the red buoy."

I said, "I'm not drowning." And he said, "You are drifting, you're in a rip current. Grab the red buoy." I could tell by the tone of his voice that I had better grab on. So, I did, and he swam to shore pulling me in. I will never forget how embarrassing it was because when I got to shore. There were people standing up, applauding, clapping that he saved me. How mortified I was. So, then I began walking toward the lifeguard tower to look for my towel and my belongings, and it was all gone. I thought, *you got to be kidding me. Now somebody took all of my stuff.* I began looking and then pretty soon I realized that there were many lifeguard towers staggered across the beach.

I started walking north to the next one, and then the next one, and then the next one, and sure enough there's all of my stuff. I failed to realize is that I was in a rip current and had drifted all that way without even knowing because I was not on solid ground. I had no anchor. I had nothing to gauge my position.

And so, the moral of that story is that we must be very careful at times because we may be drifting away from our purpose, our mission, and not even realize it. And when someone tries to call our attention to help us, or they try to throw us a lifeline, and oftentimes we ignore it, so I encouraged him to stay grounded and be careful not to ever drift. Jelly thought the story was good and we talked about what he was anchored to in his life. His primary anchor, was to the Lord, then his family, friends, and soccer in that order. Amazing to hear him reflect.

During our Project Kawthoolei 2017–2018, we would often encounter young people playing soccer in the camps and villages. Each time I saw them, I thought about Jelly Poe. and If he had been able to accompany us on this trip, he would have challenged everyone with his skill and passion for soccer. I would share his story with many who also were passionate about soccer. They would be very quiet as I shared the story of Jelly Poe.

Jelly would teach me so much about competition, and the important of being our best at everything we do. He was so humble, yet, I could see in him such an amazing drive for playing soccer at his best. He knew he was so good at soccer, yet his right leg would be taken from him. But it seemed as if he knew all this was a part of God's plan, so God could shine His love through the life of Jelly Poe.

Jelly was so bold in sharing with me how his life would be an example for many to see how God was the most important thing for every person. He would frequently tell me how he knew for absolute certainty that the Lord loved him, held him in His mighty hand, and that Jelly trusted God with all his heart. He knew that God was in control, and Jelly would share with me that one day many will likely face a similar fate. Jelly would encourage me to rise up and not be afraid.

I was so taken back, because I could sense that none of this was an accident. God would use Jelly to draw me in and teach me before he would leave this earth. I was so humbled, never experiencing anything even close to this. Jelly was sharing a message with me that I knew was preparing me for a work God would have for me later to serve the Karen people. I was scared, yet, comforted, it is so difficult to explain. One thing after another would lead me to recognize that I would be standing in the gap for the Karen and that I must rise up to this calling. Jelly would be my inspiration, my little brother leading from the front, by example.

I knew Jelly as experiencing the fight for his life, yet, he was consumed with teaching me, and being present and focused on making sure that I understood that there was a greater purpose for my life and that it would be to stand with his people!

Chapter Seven

Jelly Experiences Adversity

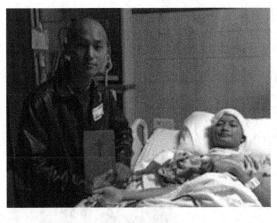

Jelly was the happy-go-lucky kid! Everything always seemed to go his way. Yet, Jelly was going to experience some very tough times, times that for most people, would cause them to fall, to question God, to question everything. Yet, Jelly, navigated through this storm like a pro. The adversity he would begin to experience would challenge everyone around Jelly, yet for Jelly, it seemed as though he was unfazed. He knew there was a play for his life, and he did not question anything that was happening to him.

In 2015, Jelly began experiencing pain on his right knee. He was 14-years-old. He was taken to the doctor where they believed if he stayed off his leg, it would get better. They did not do the tests that might have revealed an early diagnosis of cancer. Jelly rested his leg for a while, and then he began playing soccer again. Jelly was so passionate about soccer and could not wait to get back on the field, the sooner the better.

Months later, Jelly noticed the pain return to his right knee. This time, it was worse. X-rays revealed a tumor, and this time the doctors did the appropriate tests. It revealed the worst, Jelly had osteosarcoma cancer. It is the most common type of cancer that develops in bone and is one of the most aggressive forms. Like the osteoblasts in normal bone, the cells that form this cancer make

bone matrix. But the bone matrix of an osteosarcoma is not as strong as that of normal bones. Most osteosarcoma occur in children and young adults.

If the disease is localized, meaning it has not spread to other areas of the body, the long-term survival rate is 70 to 75 percent. However, if osteosarcoma has already spread to the lungs or other bones at diagnosis, the long-term survival rate is about 30 percent.

The doctors immediately began treating Jelly with chemotherapy, treating him with Methotrexate, given in high doses along with Leucovorin to prevent side effects. However, these drugs did not have the impact needed to reduce Jelly's highly malignant cancer. Maybe if the doctor had checked Jelly for cancer during the first appointment, possibly it could have been caught in time. However, this cancer was still aggressively moving through Jelly's leg and body.

Throughout this ordeal, Jelly remained positive and optimistic, committing himself to embrace the Lord and be positive, even when he learned later on that his right leg would have to be amputated in an effort to try to stop the cancer.

Jelly's family and friends drew ever so close to him.

Jelly knew the love they had for him, and moreover, Jelly knew that God was in control, and nothing could happen to him that he and God could not handle together.

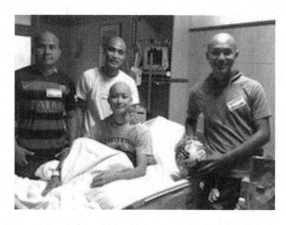

As time passed, a scan showed the cancer spreading into his lungs. Jelly was told that the treatment was not working. He also overheard the doctors saying he had maybe six weeks to live. Jelly went into hospice care in 2017 which meant that medical professionals would no longer aggressively try to fight the cancer. Rather, the treatment would be palliative care to make him as comfortable as possible. Caring would take precedence over curing. Typically, when a person is placed in hospice, the longest estimate for their life is six months.

Jelly, now attending high school was asked if he wanted to continue going to his school. The Sunday before school was to start, while completing the forms, Jelly prayed to God, as he said the pain was so bad for him to sit up. It was becoming harder to breathe because the cancer had spread into his lungs.

The local Make-a-Wish foundation made it possible for Jelly to attend a professional soccer game as well as giving him the opportunity to meet all the players on both teams. They also afforded he and his family the opportunity to go to the zoo together.

Jelly wanted to just spend as much time as possible with family and friends. His dad, Moh L. Poe, had to grapple with the fact that his firstborn would be taken before learning how to drive a car, before graduating high school, before going to college, or even getting married. So Moh decided to teach Jelly how to drive. He didn't want Jelly to miss out on that experience. Jelly learned to drive the car as naturally as one could imagine, as the videos on his dad's cell phone

demonstrated.

Keep in mind that the family was going through some very difficult times not just because of Jelly's cancer but dealing with the challenge of not knowing or understanding all the details because of the language barrier. Some members of the community meant well in trying to do as much as possible for Jelly and his family, but Jelly and his parents wanted to make their own choices and have full autonomy in any decision they took. They described feeling smothered by some community members that felt they knew what was best for Jelly rather that his own parents.

At first, family hovered close to Jelly. Then friends who loved Jelly surrounded him because Jelly had so touched their lives. He never complained; he always tried to put on his best face and stayed positive. Jelly fully trusted God with his future, whatever that future might hold. While under hospice care in the hospital, Jelly often shared that he loved listening to the songs "Trust in You" by Lauren Daigle and "Going Home" by Chris Tomlin. Everyone said that he put all others first and that he would be last . . . always.

Jenna Delaney Gibbons shared that her mom reflected that every time she spoke with Jelly or texted with Jelly he would say that he was fine, even as he was going through his fight with cancer. He would always change the conversation to "How are *you?*" He always thought of others and always tried to keep a smile on his face.

Jelly constantly showed his strength. I would want to cry many times, and Jelly would look deep in my eyes penetrating my heart, and I would see that there was something greater inside of him talking to me. Jelly was facing such difficult times, yet his example appeared to be directed right at me. He was suffering, but he would look deep into my eyes, smile, and say, "It's OK, sir, don't be sad." I was overwhelmed with emotion that a fourteen-year-old boy, with more courage than I had ever seen, was gently teaching me for what I could sense was a deeper purpose.

I would cry out to the Lord as I would drive to the local drugstore to get supplies for Jelly, praying "Lord, please help Jelly!" I would feel nothing in response and return back to his house, with Jelly gently looking at me saying, "It's OK, sir, don't cry." I would be awed, thinking, *who is this Jelly Poe?*

Chapter Eight

Jelly's Final Days on This Earth

By 2017, Jelly Poe, a refugee from Karen State, had been battling osteosarcoma for more than a year. And he had been under hospice care at home.

I had come to know Jelly from his admiration of our PowerMentor program and our medical outreach efforts each year to his country. He began communicating with me on Facebook expressing appreciation for helping his people. Through various posts, I knew that Jelly had his leg amputated in an effort to stop the cancer and that he was fourteen-years-old when he lost his leg. I knew that he was in the final stages of his battle with cancer.

Jelly asked me if he could meet me in person. It

really hit my heart, so I scheduled a flight and told him I would be there in three days. He told me he was going to try and hang on until I got there. I noted how gracious he was, always so thankful for all the things that people have been doing for him. And it was evident he had such a close-knit family, which is typical for the Karen people.

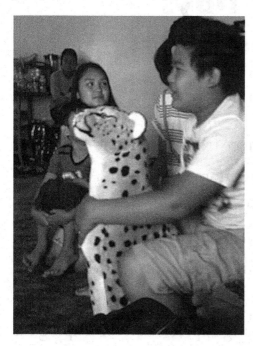

On Friday, August 25, 2017, I departed San Diego for Nashville, Tennessee. I had Wi-Fi while in the air and was messaging with Jelly who was so excited that I was coming. He would tell me that I was his hero; yet, I would tell him that he was my hero and that I was so awed by his courage. Prior to my departure, he told me about his younger sister and two brothers. I asked him what kind of a gift he would he like to give each of them, so they could remember him. He chose a soccer ball for his twelve-year-old sister, Hen Nay Thaw, an oversized stuffed cheetah for his nine-year-old brother, Lah Bywe Htoo, and a race car for his four-year-old brother, Johnantha Poe. I arranged for them to be delivered via Amazon Prime prior to my arrival. I told him, "Jelly, these gifts are from you to them as this will mean a great deal to them." He said, "Sir, that is very kind of you, thank you."

I arrived in Nashville around nine at night. When I called Jelly from the airport, he told me he was still hanging on and asked me what time I would be there. I told him it would take me about forty-five minutes to drive to his home from the airport. I drove quickly, stopping nowhere as I could sense from Jelly that he was not doing well.

When I arrived, Jelly's dad met me in the parking lot, and we hugged, and I told him what an amazing dad he was. He understood even though we had a major language barrier. He walked me into their apartment where Jelly was lying in a daybed with oxygen on in the living room. His mom and grandparents were in the living room with him. Jelly had a smile from ear to ear as did I. His body was very frail, and I had a tough time not crying. I could see he was in respiratory distress.

I sat down on his bed gave him a gentle hug and told him how privileged I was to be able to actually meet him, my hero. He smiled and then spoke softly because it was very hard for him to talk. I told him I knew that it was difficult for him to talk and I brought my iPad that he could use to communicate with me by typing notes instead of having to talk.

I showed him the guitar I brought him as he wanted to learn how to play the guitar. I played a few songs for him and showed him some basic chords he could learn. He was so happy, so grateful.

His dad had to keep repositioning Jelly in the bed to make him comfortable. With the cancer in his lungs, Jelly had a very difficult time breathing, catching his breath, and was wracked with coughing.

Jelly told me that he could not sleep at night; it was his most difficult time. I told him no worries, I was prepared to stay up with him. He asked me if he could lean on me to be comfortable, to which I told him of course. He then asked me to hold him to steady his frail body, as I played some songs for him from my iPhone.

I also noticed that his oxygen was set to three instead of five, the higher number would supply a greater amount of oxygen. I asked the family if the nurse had explained the settings to them, but they had received no instructions. Because Jelly was having such a tough time breathing, I increased it to five. I found some information in his medical paperwork that indicated it was the recommended setting.

That first night, while holding him, I would try to help him relax his breathing by playing slower music and adjusting my breathing to match his rhythm, then slowing mine so he could try to catch his breath by mimicking me. He appreciated my efforts, telling me how meaningful this was for him. I would ask him to envision us the ocean, and as the waves would come in, we would breathe to each wave. He felt that helped him and thanked me for doing that.

I asked him what he was thinking, and he said he hoped he could be healed, but he was prepared for whatever God planned. I could not help but reflect how this young boy held no anger at his situation, had complete and full trust in God's outcome for his life.

His mom and dad were awake all night as well. I wondered how many days this had been going on.

At some point during my visit, Jelly's mom gave me a box with documents dating back as far as 2015 and as current as just a few weeks old. She asked me to help her make sense of them. Then Jelly's cousin came over and began sharing with me details of the story of how all of this transpired. He shared that Jelly, an avid soccer player, began having pain on his knee in 2016. He went to the doctors, and after some test, it revealed that it was cancer. They hoped to stop the spread by amputating his leg, but it was not successful. Even after the amputation, the cancer continued to spread.

In the box, I found another document dated 2015 from a Baptist medical clinic. I showed it to Jelly and asked him why he had gone there. Jelly told me that he had noticed a sore on his leg and went to the clinic to have it examined. They told him that they removed a part of the bone and stitched him up. After they examined the bone sample, they determined that some of the bone had deteriorated.

As I began reviewing other medical records, it became obvious to me, that Jelly had signs of bone cancer in 2015, but the clinic hadn't caught it, so it continued to spread until the tumor on his knee was diagnosed in late 2016 to early 2017.

Now this aggressive cancer was in his lungs, with no hope for a cure, so Jelly was in hospice care.

Jelly's mom also brought me a large Ziploc bag full of medication and asked what they what should they be giving him. When I questioned Jelly's mom if the hospice nurse had given them instructions, she responded, "Not really." I began to realize this huge gap in communication. Jelly's family did not really know what was going on they also did not understand that hospice treatment only was to make Jelly's life as comfortable as possible in his final days.

When his brothers and sister woke up in the

morning, the Amazon Prime box had already been delivered, and it was awesome to see Jelly present each of them with the gift he chose so they could remember him all their lives.

While I was there, I witnessed Moe L. Poe, Jelly's dad, lifting his firstborn son from the daybed into a wheelchair to take him to the bathroom and for showers. I could see the excruciating pain that Jelly was in every time he had to be lifted. When I asked if hospice had provided a portable toilet that could be placed near Jelly's bed for him to use, they said no. So, I drove to a nearby Walmart and bought one. After I set it up, Jelly was so pleased that he would not have to make that journey all the way to the bathroom.

I also noticed that Jelly was using stuffed animals to prop him up in the daybed and the button eyes in different parts of some of the animals were digging into his skin causing him pain. Again, I asked if hospice had told Jelly and his family that Jelly could be provided with a hospital bed that could be adjusted into different positions, and yet again they said no. I was speechless.

I asked Jelly if he wanted a remote-controlled recliner

that he could adjust as needed in order to breathe more easily. And he said, "Yes, sir, that would be great."

His dad and I went to a local furniture store and bought a recliner and took it back to the apartment. Jelly was so happy that he could sit in the recliner and have the autonomy to remotely position himself whenever he wanted.

I noticed Jelly's skin in some areas were scaling, and so I bought lotion and showed his mom and dad how to massage his leg, arms, chest, and back using the lotion, which would also moisturize his skin, and improve circulation. Jelly said that it felt so good to have the massages and the lotion on his skin. I bought a massager because Jelly really liked to have his leg and his back massaged, and if his dad used the machine, the massages were more effective.

I asked Jelly if he wanted to clean his mouth, to which he said yes; so, I used some disposable toothbrushes to clean his mouth. However, he told me that his mouth was sensitive. I asked if hospice had supplied him with mouth swabs, and yet again his family said no. I ordered some swabs from Amazon Prime, which were delivered later that same day.

All these gaps in care troubled me. I realized that Jelly and his family did not understand what hospice care meant and what resources were available to them. In addition, I noticed some people from outside of the Karen community would drop by to say hi and show their support. I also noted that Jelly's dad has not been going to work so he could stay with his son. When I asked him if anyone was helping them financially, he said no. The rent was $650 a month. I made a post on Facebook asking for help, and immediately funds began pouring in to pay almost two months' rent for the family. It was sad to know that with many coming by for support, some may not have known that the Poe family had monetary needs to pay bills.

On Sunday, Jelly asked me why I was not taking pictures with him. I shared that when my mom passed away months ago, my mom was sensitive to have photos taken of her when she was at her worst. Instead, I wanted her to be remembered by photos of her in better condition. I would even touch up the photos to smooth them in attempt to make her look her best. But Jelly's mindset was completely different. He told me, "Sir, it's OK to take photos with me when I am at my worst. I want everyone to see that at my worst, I am still able to be at my best." I did not know how to respond. I was speechless. I kissed his forehead and said with tears, "Jelly, you teach me so much, do you know that?" He said, "Yes, sir, thank you."

A few other things happened that I want to mention because I saw the challenges the family faced. I hope no one takes offense to what I'm going to describe, but this is what transpired. On Saturday, a large group of seven or eight Jehovah's Witnesses came to the Poe family door. I could tell they had been there before, so I figured everything was fine with the family when they invited themselves in. They began trying to talk to Jelly, who was very weak, showing him their materials and asking him questions. This went on for several hours and they would not take a hint to leave. I was reluctant to intervene because I did not know if this was something the family wanted. Jelly told me he was tired, so I stepped in and told them that Jelly needed to rest. Then the Jehovah Witnesses sat on the floor and ate lunch with Jelly's family and stayed a total time of almost three hours. After they left, I explained to Jelly's parents that this was really taxing on Jelly and that I would not recommend they allow strangers into their home. Jelly wanted to be surrounded by family and close friends not people who were there for their own purposes. In addition, I learned that some Mormons had also been coming and had been very assertive in pushing their beliefs. In addition to the Jehovah Witnesses and Mormons, Jelly's family's pastor was also coming over on a regular basis, which brought tremendous comfort to them. You can imagine how overwhelming and confusing it must have been for Jelly and his family to have people from different faiths coming over to proselytize their beliefs and not feel they could tell them all to leave. The time remaining to spend with Jelly was so limited. How terribly difficult for them to have all these other people around who were more interested in pushing their beliefs than comforting and respecting Jelly and his family.

That Sunday, I departed around 11:30 a.m. to head to the airport. It was very hard to say good-bye to Jelly. We had talked before about the fact that I would see him in heaven one day and we would hang out. I knew this would be the last time I would see him on this earth. He and I would look into each other's eyes, both knowing this was our last in person meeting time. As I left we both had tear filled eyes. I walked out to the rental car to leave.

Not three minutes later, I received a call from Jelly's dad saying that his son's breathing was very labored, and the family was scared. They did not know what to do. I turned around and returned to the house.

When I arrived, I could see Jelly was in respiratory distress. Immediately, I went to his side, began talking to him in an effort to help him catch his breath. The family called hospice, and a hospice nurse arrived in about a half an hour.

When the hospice nurse came, a few things concerned me. In front of his family, she asked Jelly if he wanted to be taken to the hospital so that they could give him lots of love. How could she even say something like that to him? Obviously, Jelly could find no greater love than that from his family, in their home.

The nurse looked through the things that she left behind from her previous visit. She noticed all the supplies that we had now: the mouth swabs I had bought, the lotion, the massager, the recliner, and portable toilet. Then she had the nerve to remark that we didn't have to purchase those things on our own; they could have been supplied by hospice if we had just asked. I quickly said the problem was that hospice hadn't provided Jelly with all the supplies he needed for adequate care and he should have had all those things the minute he went into hospice care. She just smiled and thanked me for my generosity.

Then the nurse sort of amped things up by sharing with some family members that she would like to take Jelly to the hospital. I could see Jelly was getting scared. He started to cry. I embraced him and said, "We have our arms around you on this side, and God has His arms waiting for you on the other side. You are in good hands my little brother." I shared with him how much he had set my heart on fire for his vision for my supporting the Karen people that he so worried about. He smiled and said, "Thank you sir!" Then the hospice nurse administered some morphine so that Jelly was able to go to sleep and his breathing relaxed.

I then departed for the airport. Before leaving Jelly, his mom and dad lay down on his bed with Jelly in the middle, as they held him, and comforted him. How powerful it was to see Jelly surrounded by his mom and dad having their special intimate time with their firstborn.

While I was on the flight back to San Diego, Jelly had woken up and messaged me to thank me for everything I had done for him and his family. I told him how much he impacted my life and what an incredibly courageous hero he was for me. He said that he chose to stay home and not go to the hospital, which I was very relieved to hear that.

His mom and dad stayed in communication with me to keep me posted during the following days. On August 30, 2017 he passed away early in the morning on his 15th birthday, just as he had said would be the day he would go to be with the Lord.

When I look back on the last couple of years in Jelly's short life, my thoughts are filled with questions. What if the doctors had done a test to understand why his bone was deteriorating? Would he still be alive today? Given the fact that he was only thirteen years old when the pain in his leg first manifested itself, why weren't they aggressive in determining a diagnosis? Why were there so many gaps in his care? In his treatment? Why didn't hospice provide Jelly and his family with adequate instructions for his care? Why didn't they give Jelly all he needed to make his last months on Earth as comfortable and peaceful as possible? Why didn't they ask for translators to help? So many questions . . . so many lessons learned.

When Jenna Delaney Gibbons, his teacher, found out Jelly was so sick, she was blessed to have the chance to spend time with him and his family for several weeks leading up to his passing. Jelly and his family were able to come to her farm and loved being near their horses. Jelly truly enjoyed a little horse therapy. During one of her last visits with him, she knew she had to tell him how much he changed her life. Jenna told him that he

was the sweetest young man she had ever met, and that she hoped her son, Rowan, would grow up to be like Jelly one day. She told him he gave her

hope for the future, that young people would look to him as an example of true kindness, compassion, courage, politeness, and determination. Above all, Jelly's faith had inspired everyone to trust in God's love for us. It's amazing to Jenna how one young man had such an impact on so many people. Jelly changed her life. Jenna aches for him today, but she knows he is with the Lord.

Jenna recounted her last text to Jelly, "I love you, we all love you, and above all God loves you." Jelly sweetly wrote back, "Yes, ma'am, and I love you, too."

Often, during my visit with Jelly, I would ask him what he felt God was doing. He said, "Sir, I hope he heals me, and I know He could, but if not, I trust Him with my life." Jelly had made his preparations to meet God. He and I sang songs on that last weekend of his life on this earth. He would tell me how much pain he was in, yet he continued to have his legendary smile.

Jelly never spoke about his prognosis even when he was in hospice care. He did tell many that he wanted to be with the Lord on his fifteenth birthday. Did he know that would come to fruition?

Chapter Nine

Jelly, the Influencer

Jelly had the ability to influence others in such a subtle way. In his ever so gentle tone, Jelly's words penetrated very deeply into the hearts of many.

Htoo Aye, Jelly's fellow Karen friend shared his startling dream about Jelly Poe. Htoo had dreamed this after Jelly passed away. In his dream, Jelly was lying down; he was still alive. Htoo described how hard it was for him to watch. When he woke up, he realized Jelly's funeral had already happened a few weeks ago. It impacted him intensely, leaving him feeling very sad, but thankful that Jelly led such an influential life, and recognized how much Jelly inspired and impacted him, yet he only knew him through messages on Facebook messaging. Te Nee, who knew Jelly, also described a dream he had in the beginning of October 2017. He and his brother were playing with Jelly and Te remarked that Jelly was not sick, and he was just like before, and they were just playing like kids do.

Tee Soe would also describe a dream that he had about Jelly Poe playing soccer in the park.

As I travel the United States visiting Karen communities, as Jelly had asked me to do, I share the story of Jelly Poe, and without exception, every time I share his story, most are drawn to tears, even those who had not every met him.

During a visit to Minnesota in the fall of 2017, I was joined by our PowerMentor Leadership team consisting of Tee Soe, Samuel Sher, and Htoo Aye. The four of us conducted some leadership workshops for the Karen living there. During the workshop, I shared the story of Jelly Poe, and many were drawn to tears. I shared with them the concern that Jelly had for his Karen people. Later that night, on October 1, 2017, the four of us were staying with Samuel Sher's family, and we began talking about the concern over all the attention in the world focused on the Rohingya situation in Burma, while neglecting the Karen, Kachin, Shan, and other ethnic nationalities in the region under attack by the Burmese army. I had recently learned that there was legislation working its way through the Myanmar congress to reinstate sanctions against the Burmese army, however as I read through some drafts, I noted that it only focused on the Rohingya. This really concerned me. Having Jelly in mind, I thought about it what Jelly told me, "Sir, please never give up on my Karen people…" Whenever I would reflect on his words, my eyes would well up with tears. I recalled the time Jelly would tell me that he could envision something big that we would bring all the Karen people together for something special to unite all the Karen people.

A vision came to my mind while reflecting on Jelly's words, *what if we were able to gather ten thousand Karen people in Washington, DC, to influence Congress and help them see the greatness of the Karen people, ask for inclusion of the ethnic nationalities by name, and really make this a historic event.* Could this be the vision Jelly had of a large gathering of his Karen people? I had a gut feeling I do not even know where the ten thousand number came from. As I shared this with the team, Tee Soe,

said, let's get this on video right now. Tee is a man of action, and he did not want this moment to escape our grip.

We made a video sharing with the Karen people of our desire to have a Karen Day in DC, and we began organizing the effort. As we collaborated with Dai Lai Htoo from the Karen Organization of the United States,

we could see that this was something outside of ourselves—it was destined for the Karen people. The Karen would come to the capital of the United States to share who they are, make their historic presence known. We would be very careful to make sure this would not be a protest, nor a demonstration. Every time someone called it that, we were quick to correct them. This would be a day to

celebrate the amazing Karen and introduce them to the world with the U.S. Capitol Building as the backdrop. Dai Lai would arrange for Karen dancers to perform at the event. Jelly would be the inspiration for us!

I submitted a permit for the event to the appropriate authorities, and we began to craft the agenda. This would be a time the Karen would share their gratefulness

for the United States and all they have done around the world. We would highlight the great things the Karen people have brought to the United States, but then . . . We would also make a strong statement about the Karen suffering in Kawthoolei, the Burmese Army's continual incursion into Karen territory and ask the United States to intervene and force the Burmese army to stop their attacks on the ethnic nationalities in the region. I would pray and ask God to honor this time and help us make this happen. I imagined having a conversation with Jelly and saying, "Jelly, I wish you were here for this, because we are going to do something big and stand for your Karen people. I will tell the crowd your story, Jelly, so young people can see you as their role model."

On Saturday night, while in Philadelphia, we would speak to a large group of young people, and I would share about Jelly and his character. I would share that Jelly knew he had six weeks to live, and he chose to have as much positive impact on those around him as he possibly could. I asked the audience, "If you knew you had six weeks to live, what would you do with your life? How would you make your life count, because, for Jelly, it was six weeks of suffering, and he had all the reason to be mad and upset with the Lord, yet, he chose to be selfless and encourage others." I shared anecdotal stories of Jelly, and as was almost always the case, many shed tears as I shared the story of Jelly Poe. Many knew him from Facebook, and those that did not know him, quickly admired him from the stories of his life.

I noted that when I spoke of Jelly I would be overcome with emotion, but in a good way, and I would find comfort knowing Jelly was with the Lord, but it also gave me purpose because of what Jelly had shared with me. He believed that I was called to serve the Karen people, and he would ask me, "Sir, please do not give up on my Karen people." I promised him I would never give up, and he told me, "Thank you, sir, I know you love our people, but it will be hard sometimes." I understood, but was committed to keeping my promise, not only to Jelly, but to the amazing Karen people.

During our project for Kawthoolei in 2017 and 2018, Jelly would lead the effort in spirit. This would be the first year to award the Jelly Poe Leadership Award. His presence was felt the entire trip because everyone knew who he was and what he valued. His character would guide our decisions and our focus.

An example of our passion that stemmed from Jelly can be found in a situation involving a five-year-old boy in Ei Htu Hta IDP (Individually Displaced People) camp whom we had treated for malaria, and more than three weeks of high fever. I want you to hear this story and see how God orchestrates amazing things. And some might assert these things were coincidences, but we know there is simply no way that this was all coincidences. Initially, we were advised that the five-year-old boy was brought to the clinic because they had not been able to break his fever and it had been 104°F for nineteen days, and even with a saline IV, the fever had not broken.

The medics at the clinic weren't sure exactly what was wrong with him. They didn't have at their disposal all the different types of IV medicine. We were able to provide some IV fluids with sodium chloride, which is what finally broke the fever, stabilizing him for transport. The parents needed 5,000 baht (comparable to $159 USD), to get him on a boat that would take him to a clinic in Mae La Oo. The parents also needed food. And we wanted to make sure that the young boy would not be alone, that his family would be with him at the clinic.

The next morning, the five-year-old boy medevac'd to the clinic; his family arrived by boat. We arrived three days later to check on him. Amazingly, he was doing great. He actually received a blood transfusion, and then here's the crazy thing. We actually met the guy who gave him blood. He was a guy here at the camp, and he's actually one of the guys who's helping us here.

And, you know, we thought about the odds that we would be put at the right place at the right time, to be able to have the right medicine... To be able to provide the financial resources to get him to a higher level of care... And then that God would allow us to be connected with the very guy who donated blood to save this little boy's life... Absolutely incredible. Family's doing great. He'll be going back to his village now. We've given them money to be able to take a boat back. And so, we're really excited about that and it really energized our entire team to see how all of this happened.

Jelly had incredible influence on the lives of those

that were a part of the Kawthoolie Project team 2017. For example, our four leaders in Mae Sot, Has Lo Moo,

Moo Taw, Rain Rain, and Has Htoo really held Jelly dear to their heart. They saw everything happening in real time in Facebook as I travelled to see Jelly. For them to see how Jelly was at the forefront of our Kawthoolei Project was very powerful. Other team members Kaw Thaw Blay, Saw Poe Baw, Saw Novel, Win Aye, Mario Solomon, Nay Say, Thawda Bu, Fri Day, Thomas Main, Elizabeth Moltzau and Johnny Vo really drew close to all Jelly Poe represented. Even our leaders in the United Sates such as Florence Poba-Prieto, Eh De Gray, Samuel Thaw, Hser K. Moo, Tee Soe, Htoo Aye, Samuel Sher, Te Nee, Sar T Doh, Kaw Po Lo, Fu Ge Kaw Ku, Kaw Khu, Chit Tway, Thaw So and Carlos Ariel Gonzalez Moreno, Ethan Maxwell, Hla Ku, Saw Ehhsu, Karma Lotey, Woni Htoo, Nicky Wah, Cuong Tran, Alex Morales, Wah Gay, Sha' Ka Paw, El Dale, Me Kwabg, Poe Nee,

Pla Plo, and Aaron Hollenberg held Jelly in such high regard.

Many Karen leaders such as Dai Lai Htoo, General Nerdah Bombya, and General Baw Kyaw Heh were very proud of Jelly Poe and all he stood for.

Of particular interest to me was 14-year-old Lual Mu Lah, an amazing Karen student mentored by Htoo Aye. I would come to know Lual as I travelled around the United States. I had sent him the previous books I

had written, and his sister and Htoo Aye would send me photos of him reading the books, one after the other. What struck me about Lual, was his eerily similar personality to that of Jelly Poe. Same age, both love soccer, both extremely kind, and both with wisdom beyond their years. Lual to note when he heard me share the story of Jelly Poe. I could see it struck deep in his heart. Lual seemed to me to pick up where Jelly left off. This will be very interesting to watch his life unfold over the next few years… Lual is an amazing blessing, and when I interact with him, it feels very similar to the presence I felt with Jelly Poe.

Chapter Ten

Jelly Never Forgotten

During conversations with Jelly near the very end, I would share with him that his life would never be forgotten, because of how he lived his life for the Lord. He would always look at me with his penetrating eyes, and say, "Yes, sir, I know!"

I often heard people telling me that Jelly was so authentic. He never talked bad about others, never was manipulative, never was into gossip, was just the real deal.

This young fourteen-year-old refugee from war-torn Karen State impacted his entire community, including the police who escorted his funeral procession as they wiped tears from their eyes. Jelly passed away August 30, 2017, on his fifteenth birthday. So many caregivers were impacted by knowing Jelly. He was keenly aware of their attempts to save his life. What was the secret to his resilient positive attitude? How was he able to smile his infectious smile all the way to the end of his life?

In late November 2017, I was invited to Phoenix, Arizona, to speak on leadership and the family to the Karen people in the area. I thought about Jelly and had a message that I knew would resonate with my audience. I shared how important it is to have a strong family and for young people to recognize that their parents were placed in their life for a very specific reason.

While I was there, an annual soccer tournament was also occurring. How perfect was this! Jelly was so passionate about soccer. I knew the moment was ripe to tell Jelly's story to impact the lives of hundreds. And that is exactly what happened as I shared his story and tied it to the message about the importance of the family.

My weekend in Phoenix—and Jelly's story—culminated with a large church service on Sunday, right before I was scheduled to fly out. I first shared with the congregation that the Karen people are known for strong families, strong culture, and the ability to get through anything. I shared that when I read Genesis 50:20, I was reminded that we must know that people will actively work against us, and harm us, and they will plan and conspire to do evil things. Yet, God said, whatever evil they thrown our way, God will use it for our good.

In Ephesians 6:1–4, the Scripture speaks to children saying, "Obey your parents, for this is the right. Honor your father and mother, which is the first commandment with a promise), so that all may be well with you, and that you may live long time on the earth.

"Fathers, do not provoke your children to anger, but bring them up in the discipline and instruction of the Lord" (NASB). Parents must lead your children equipping them for their God-given purpose.

For the young people, it is time for you to rise up, stand up for what your parents have taught you. Listen to what the Bible says: "Let no one look down on your youthfulness, but rather in speech, conduct, love, faith and purity, show yourself an example of those who believe" (1 Timothy 4:12 NASB).

1 Timothy 4:12 tells us that we are not to treat the youth as though they are unimportant. Instead, we

must be an example to them with our words, actions, love, faith, read scriptures to them, teach them how to use their gifts which are God given talent to them.

"So then, while we have opportunity, let us do good to all people, and especially to those who are of the household of the faith" (Galatians 6:10, NASB).

"Vindicate the weak and fatherless; / Do justice to the afflicted and destitute. / Rescue the weak and needy; / Deliver *them* out of the hand of the wicked" (Psalm 82:3–4, NASB),

"Be strong and courageous! Do not tremble or be dismayed; for the Lord your God is with you wherever you go" (Joshua 1:9, NASB).

These verses were many that Jelly shared with me, and I had already held dear in my heart for years. They so penetrated my heart when I could see the same verses dear to my heart, were also dear to Jelly Poe.

Kawthoolei Project, 2017–2018

As I mentioned before, this year, our Kawthoolei Project was dedicated to Jelly Poe. Before Jelly passed away, I told him I would wear his PowerMentor ID card proudly and represent him on our team. I also told

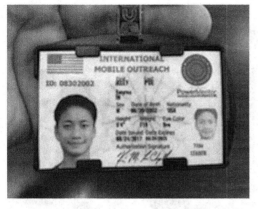

him that this would be the first time we would award someone the Jelly Poe Leadership Award. I explained that the team would vote for the one that emulated Jelly Poe's values.

Jelly rode shotgun on this trip. He was at the forefront as we openly discussed him and who he was, what he stood for, and shared how much he impacted the world around him. I could sense how much Jelly's presence was felt by the entire team. I would feel proud to wear his ID badge and would see many gazing at his photo on the ID.

One of the proudest moments was at the end of the trip when the team voted for the winner of the Jelly Poe Leadership Award. The team took this very seriously. Before they voted, we reviewed the noted character of Jelly Poe, his kindness, his love for God and his Karen people. The mood was somber as all desired to win this prestigious award. The team began writing their nomination on a little piece of paper as I walked around gather them all. As I would go through each vote, I would reflect on that team member and how I could see them emulating Jelly Poe throughout the trip. Two individuals came out on top, by large margins. The top vote went to Hso

Lo Moo, the PowerMentor leader in Mae Sot. The second highest went to Kaw Tha Blay, our medic.

As I shared their names as the winner and runner-up, the team broke out in applause. They were so pleased with the results. Hsa Lo Moo

would share what this meant to him to receive this award, and he shared that his award would remain in the PowerMentor office in Mae Sot for all to see. Kaw Tha Blay was awarded the jigsaw puzzle that contained a collage of photos from the Karen Day in Washington, DC, November 6, 2017, and the other side had the Karen flag. He would share that he wanted the puzzle to remain at the office as well so that all could reflect on the importance of a united Karen people.

The puzzle was of great significance, because as I traveled throughout the United States to Karen communities, and in Kawthoolei, I would use this puzzle to talk about the different Karen groups that often are at odds with one another. As I put the puzzle together showing the collage of the Karen Day in DC, I would share that I met Karen people from many different groups, and at the end, I would lift up the clear Plexiglas that I put the puzzle together on, to reveal on the underside the Karen flag, and that when everyone is united, the have their one flag, and this was very meaningful to the Karen people.

Each year, we will look forward to continuing our

efforts with the amazing Karen people, and along the way, give the Jelly Poe Leadership Award every year to the most deserving person who emulates the values that were so important to Jelly Poe.

Printed in the United States
By Bookmasters